BEGINNING PIANO SOLO

THE CHARLIE BROWN COLLECTION™

CONTENTS

2 BLUE CHARLIE BROWN

4 CHARLIE BROWN THEME

9 CHRISTMAS IS COMING

12 CHRISTMAS TIME IS HERE

17 THE GREAT PUMPKIN WALTZ

20 HAPPINESS THEME

22 LINUS AND LUCY

6 LOVE WILL COME

14 PEPPERMINT PATTY

27 RED BARON

24 SKATING

30 YOU'RE IN LOVE, CHARLIE BROWN

T0116613

ISBN 978-1-4950-5165-4

HAL•LEONARD® CORPORATION

7777 W. BLUEMOUND RD. P.O. BOX 13819 MILWAUKEE, WI 53213

PEANUTS © United Feature Syndicate, Inc.
www.snoopy.com

In Australia Contact:
Hal Leonard Australia Pty. Ltd.
4 Lentara Court
Cheltenham, Victoria, 3192 Australia
Email: ausadmin@halleonard.com.au

For all works contained herein:
Unauthorized copying, arranging, adapting, recording, Internet posting, public performance, or other distribution of the printed music in this publication is an infringement of copyright. Infringers are liable under the law.

Visit Hal Leonard Online at
www.halleonard.com

BLUE CHARLIE BROWN

By VINCE GUARALDI

Copyright © 1965 LEE MENDELSON FILM PRODUCTIONS, INC.
Copyright Renewed
This arrangement Copyright © 2016 LEE MENDELSON FILM PRODUCTIONS, INC.
International Copyright Secured All Rights Reserved

CHARLIE BROWN THEME

By VINCE GUARALDI

Copyright © 1964 LEE MENDELSON FILM PRODUCTIONS, INC.
Copyright Renewed
This arrangement Copyright © 2016 LEE MENDELSON FILM PRODUCTIONS, INC.
International Copyright Secured All Rights Reserved

2
1

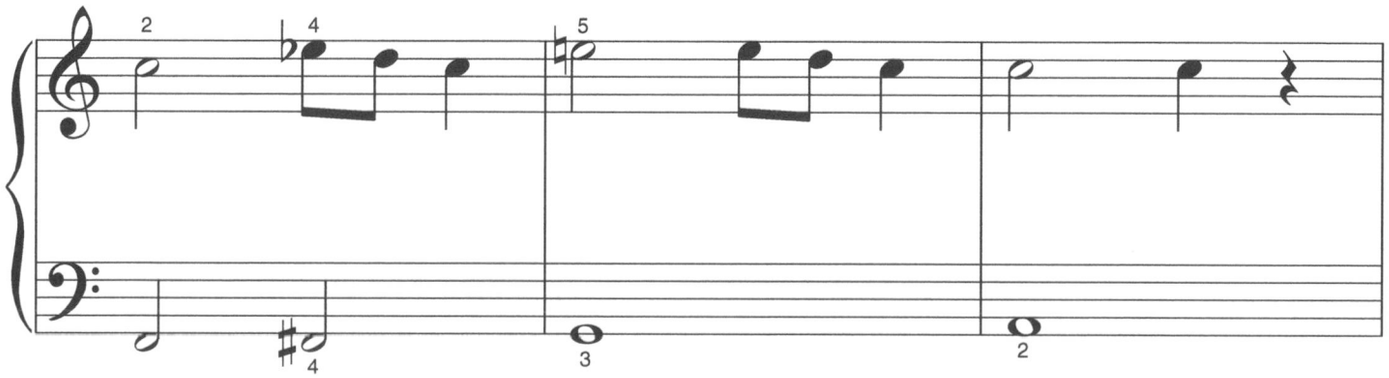
2
4
5
4
3
2

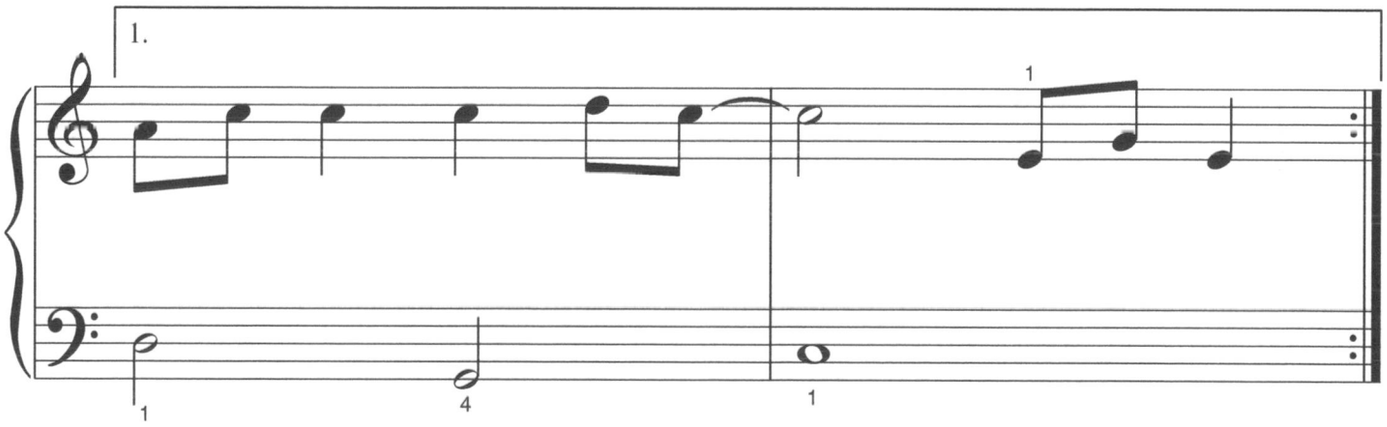
1.
1
1
4
1

2.
1
1
1
2

LOVE WILL COME

By VINCE GUARALDI

Copyright © 1967 LEE MENDELSON FILM PRODUCTIONS, INC.
Copyright Renewed
This arrangement Copyright © 2016 LEE MENDELSON FILM PRODUCTIONS, INC.
International Copyright Secured All Rights Reserved

8va

(8va)

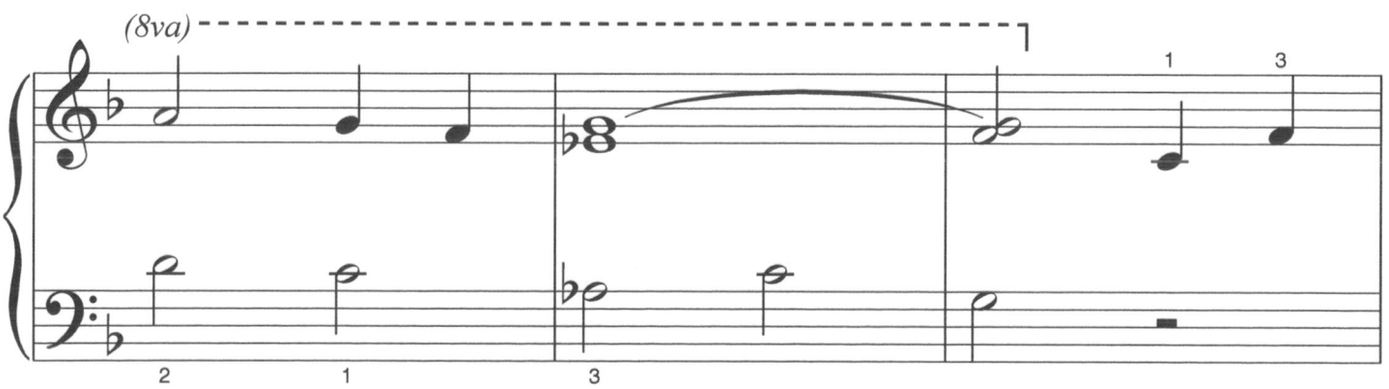
(8va)

CHRISTMAS IS COMING

from A CHARLIE BROWN CHRISTMAS

By VINCE GUARALDI

Copyright © 1966 LEE MENDELSON FILM PRODUCTIONS, INC.
Copyright Renewed
This arrangement Copyright © 2016 LEE MENDELSON FILM PRODUCTIONS, INC.
International Copyright Secured All Rights Reserved

3
4
1
3
1.
2.

CHRISTMAS TIME IS HERE

from A CHARLIE BROWN CHRISTMAS

Words by LEE MENDELSON
Music by VINCE GUARALDI

Copyright © 1966 LEE MENDELSON FILM PRODUCTIONS, INC.
Copyright Renewed
This arrangement Copyright © 2016 LEE MENDELSON FILM PRODUCTIONS, INC.
International Copyright Secured All Rights Reserved

where. Yule - tide by the fire - side and
joy - ful mem - 'ries there. Christ-mas time is here,
we'll be draw - ing near. Oh, that we could
al - ways see such spir - it through the year.

PEPPERMINT PATTY

By VINCE GUARALDI

Copyright © 1966 LEE MENDELSON FILM PRODUCTIONS, INC.
Copyright Renewed
This arrangement Copyright © 2016 LEE MENDELSON FILM PRODUCTIONS, INC.
International Copyright Secured All Rights Reserved

THE GREAT PUMPKIN WALTZ

By VINCE GUARALDI

Copyright © 1969 LEE MENDELSON FILM PRODUCTIONS, INC.
Copyright Renewed
This arrangement Copyright © 2016 LEE MENDELSON FILM PRODUCTIONS, INC.
International Copyright Secured All Rights Reserved

2
1
2
1
5
4
2
4
2
4
5
5
1
2

2
4
1
5
1
2

1.
3
5
3
3
4
5
1
5
1

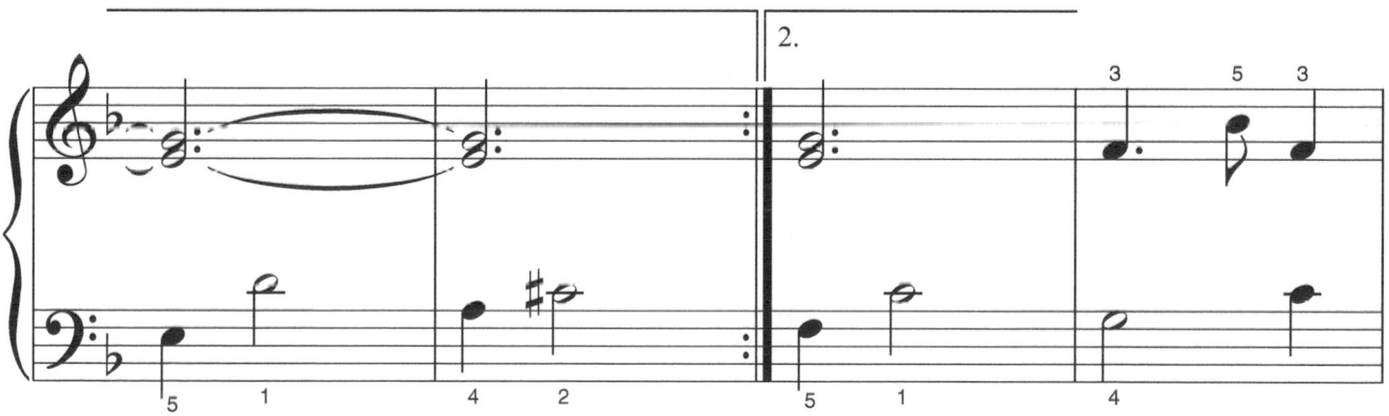
2.
5
1
4
2
5
1
3
5
3
4

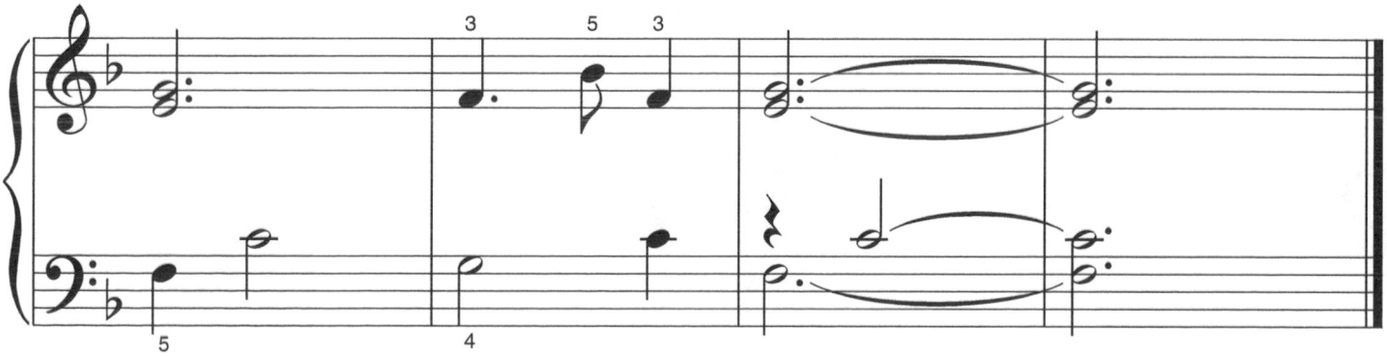
3
5
3
5
4

HAPPINESS THEME

By VINCE GUARALDI

Easy Jazz Waltz

Copyright © 1964 LEE MENDELSON FILM PRODUCTIONS, INC.
Copyright Renewed
This arrangement Copyright © 2016 LEE MENDELSON FILM PRODUCTIONS, INC.
International Copyright Secured All Rights Reserved

LINUS AND LUCY

By VINCE GUARALDI

Copyright © 1965 LEE MENDELSON FILM PRODUCTIONS, INC.
Copyright Renewed
This arrangement Copyright © 2016 LEE MENDELSON FILM PRODUCTIONS, INC.
International Copyright Secured All Rights Reserved

SKATING

By VINCE GUARALDI

Copyright © 1966 LEE MENDELSON FILM PRODUCTIONS, INC.
Copyright Renewed
This arrangement Copyright © 2016 LEE MENDELSON FILM PRODUCTIONS, INC.
International Copyright Secured All Rights Reserved

To Coda
1.
2.

D.S. al Coda
CODA
4
1
rit.

RED BARON

By VINCE GUARALDI

Copyright © 1966 LEE MENDELSON FILM PRODUCTIONS, INC.
Copyright Renewed
This arrangement Copyright © 2016 LEE MENDELSON FILM PRODUCTIONS, INC.
International Copyright Secured All Rights Reserved

To Coda

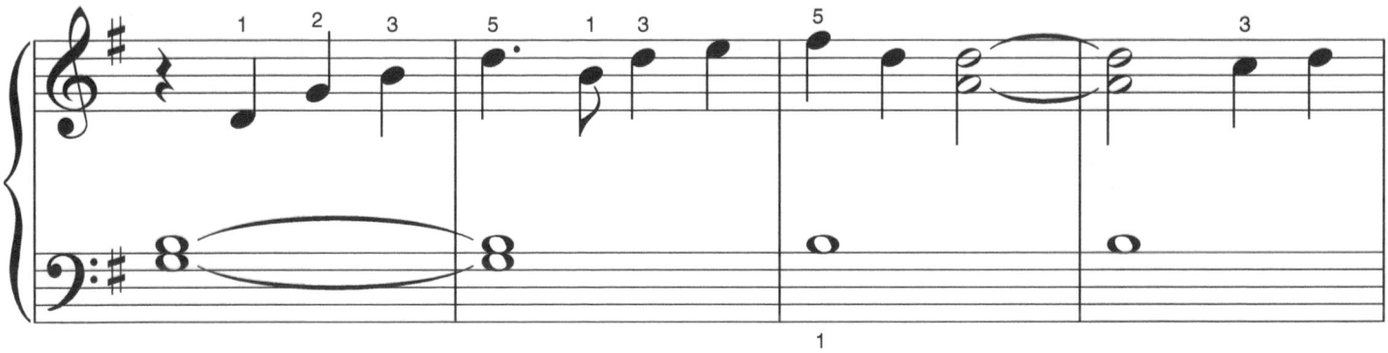

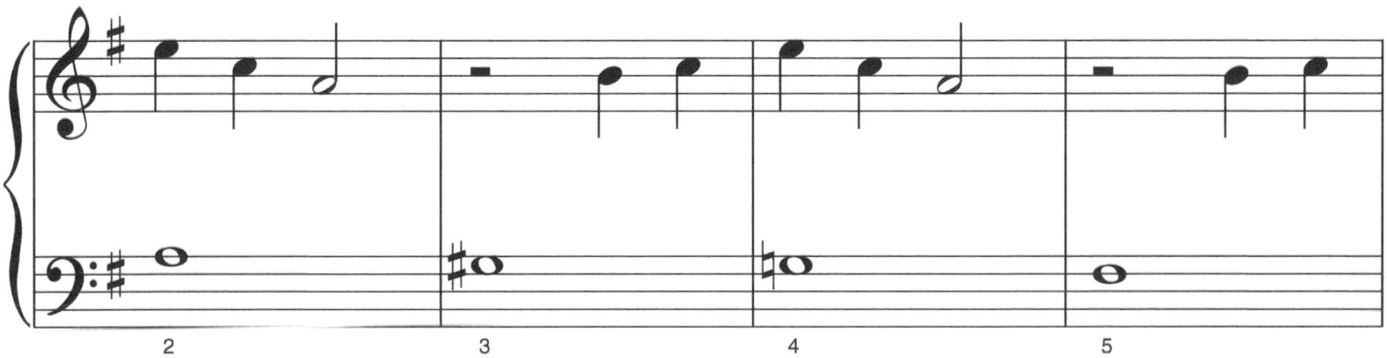

D.S. al Coda

CODA

YOU'RE IN LOVE, CHARLIE BROWN

By VINCE GUARALDI

Copyright © 1967 LEE MENDELSON FILM PRODUCTIONS, INC.
Copyright Renewed
This arrangement Copyright © 2016 LEE MENDELSON FILM PRODUCTIONS, INC.
International Copyright Secured All Rights Reserved

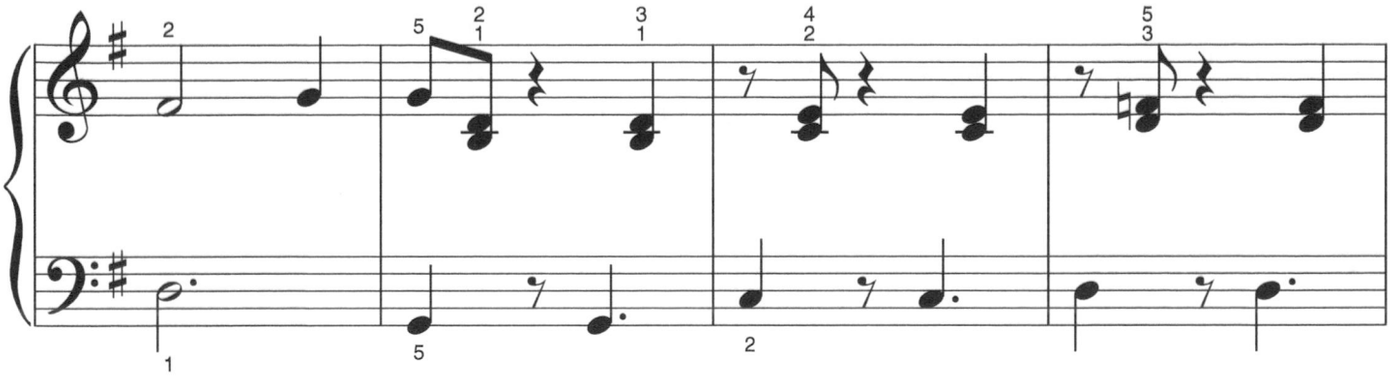

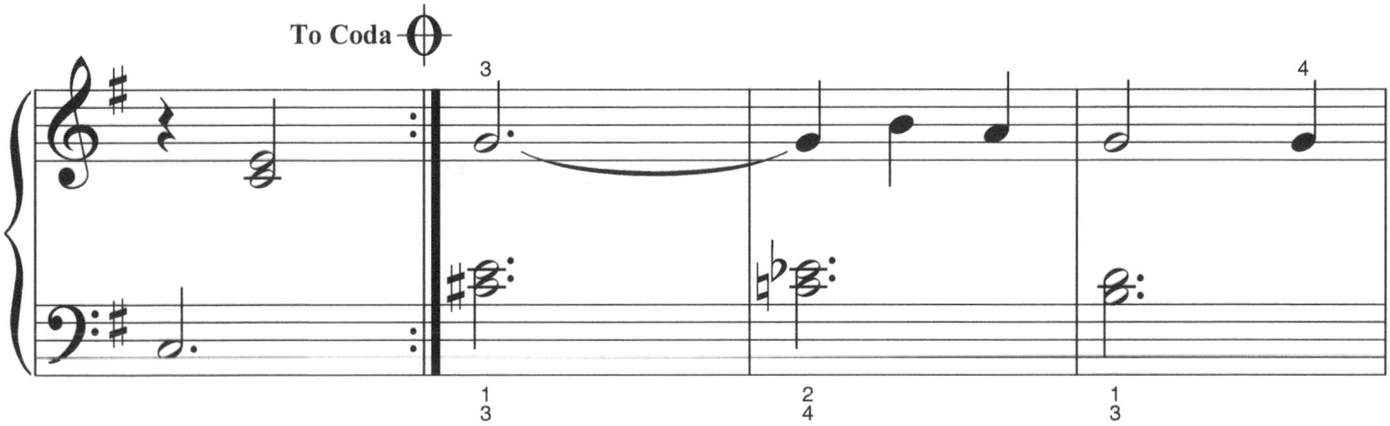
To Coda

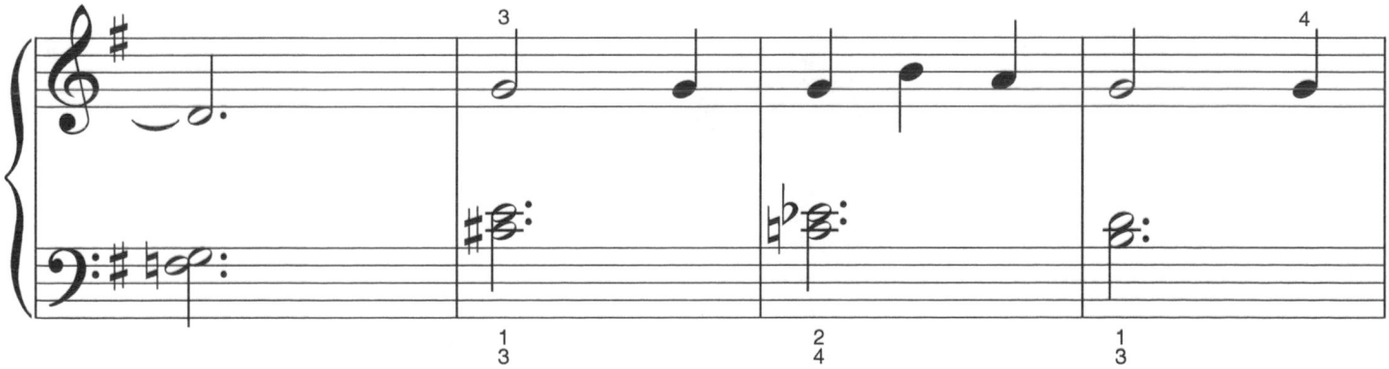

D.S. al Coda
(no repeat)
CODA